Sketa Oz Collection

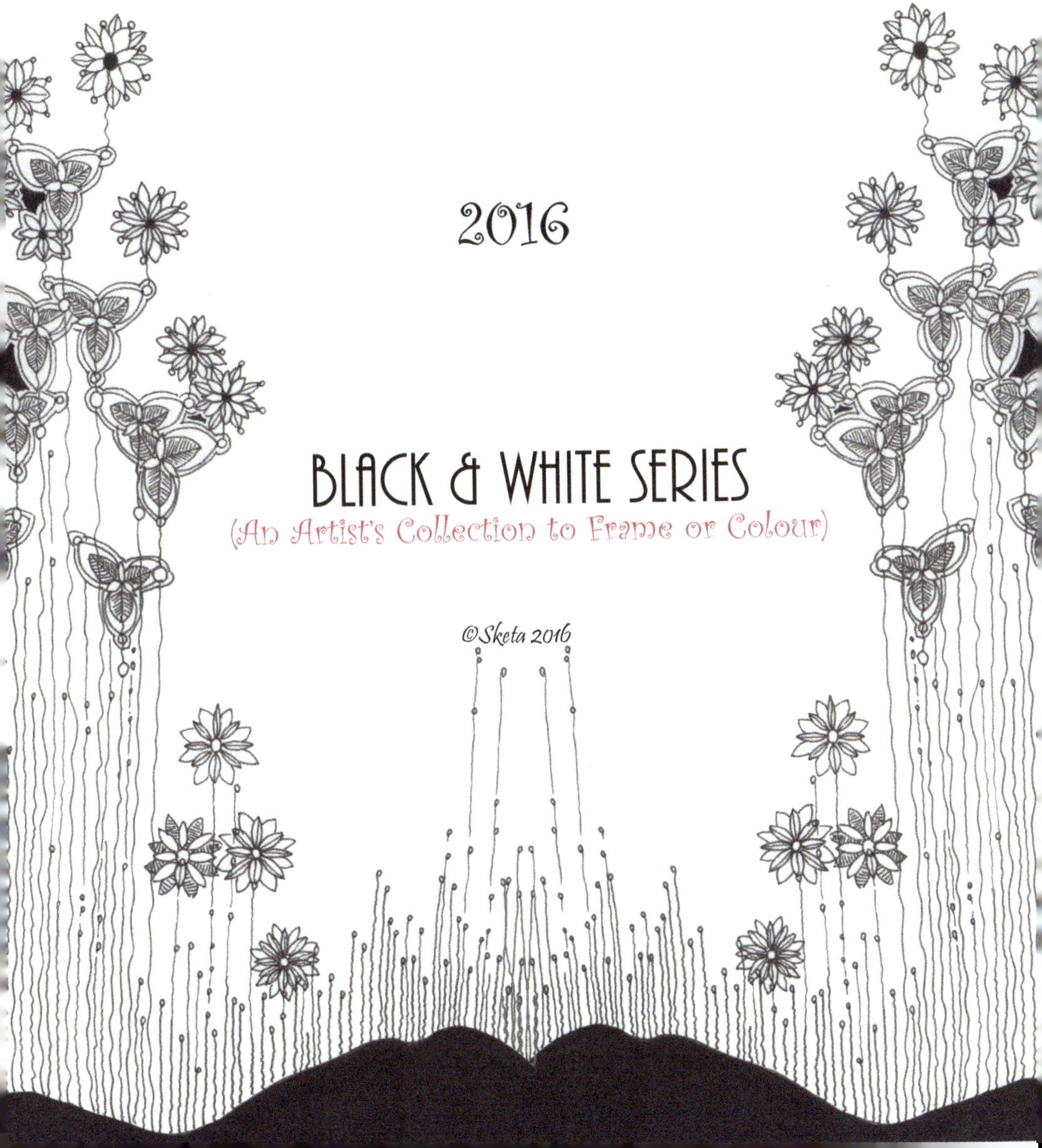

2016

BLACK & WHITE SERIES

(An Artist's Collection to Frame or Colour)

Published by ELK Publishing

www.elk-publishing.com

A catalogue record of this book is available from the Australian Library.

ISBN: 9-780994-211026

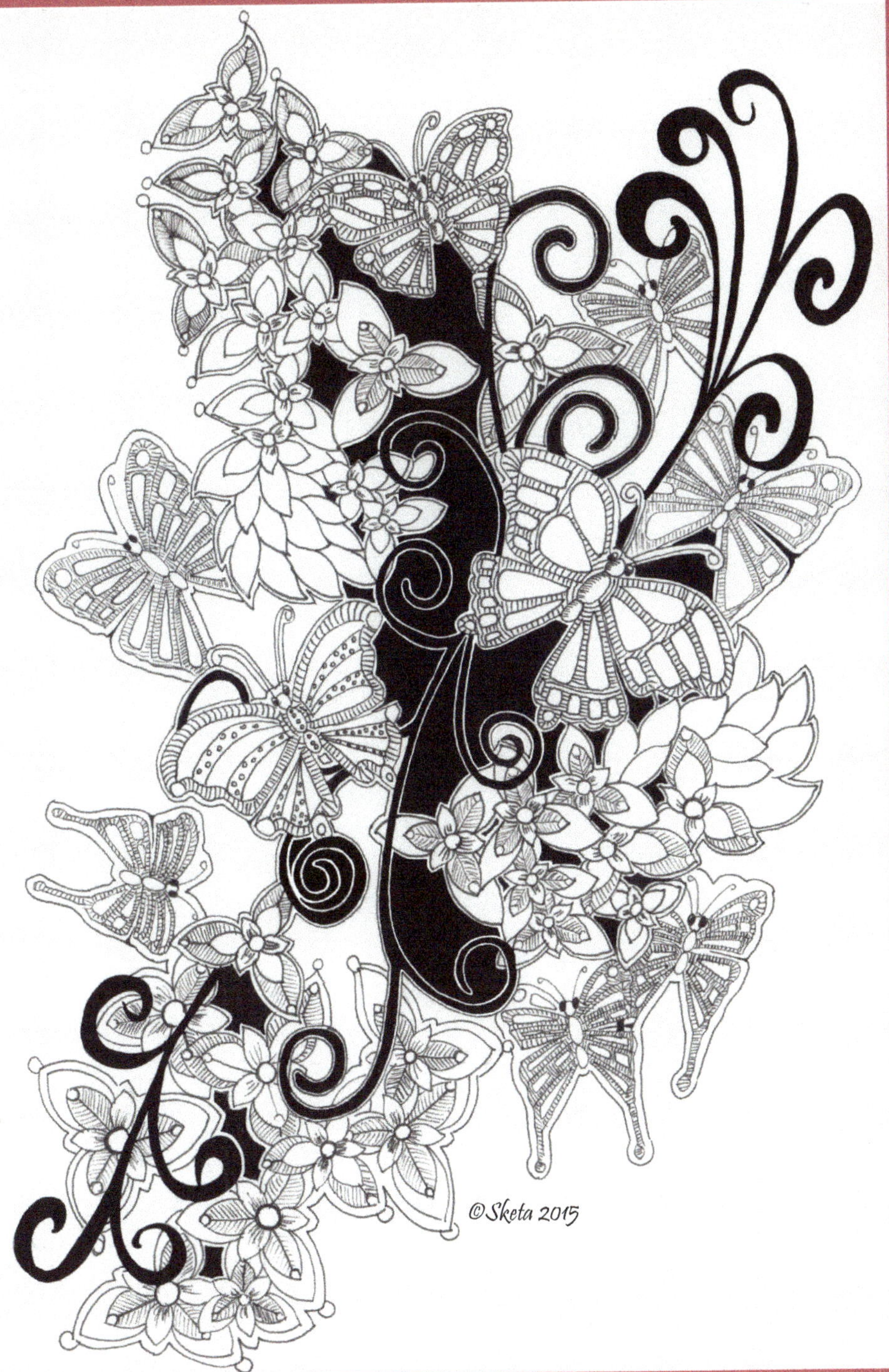
©Sketa 2015

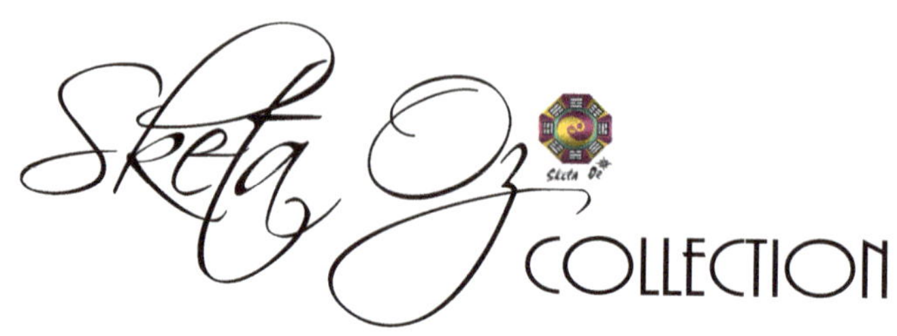

2016

BLACK & WHITE SERIES

(An Artist's Collection to Frame or Colour)

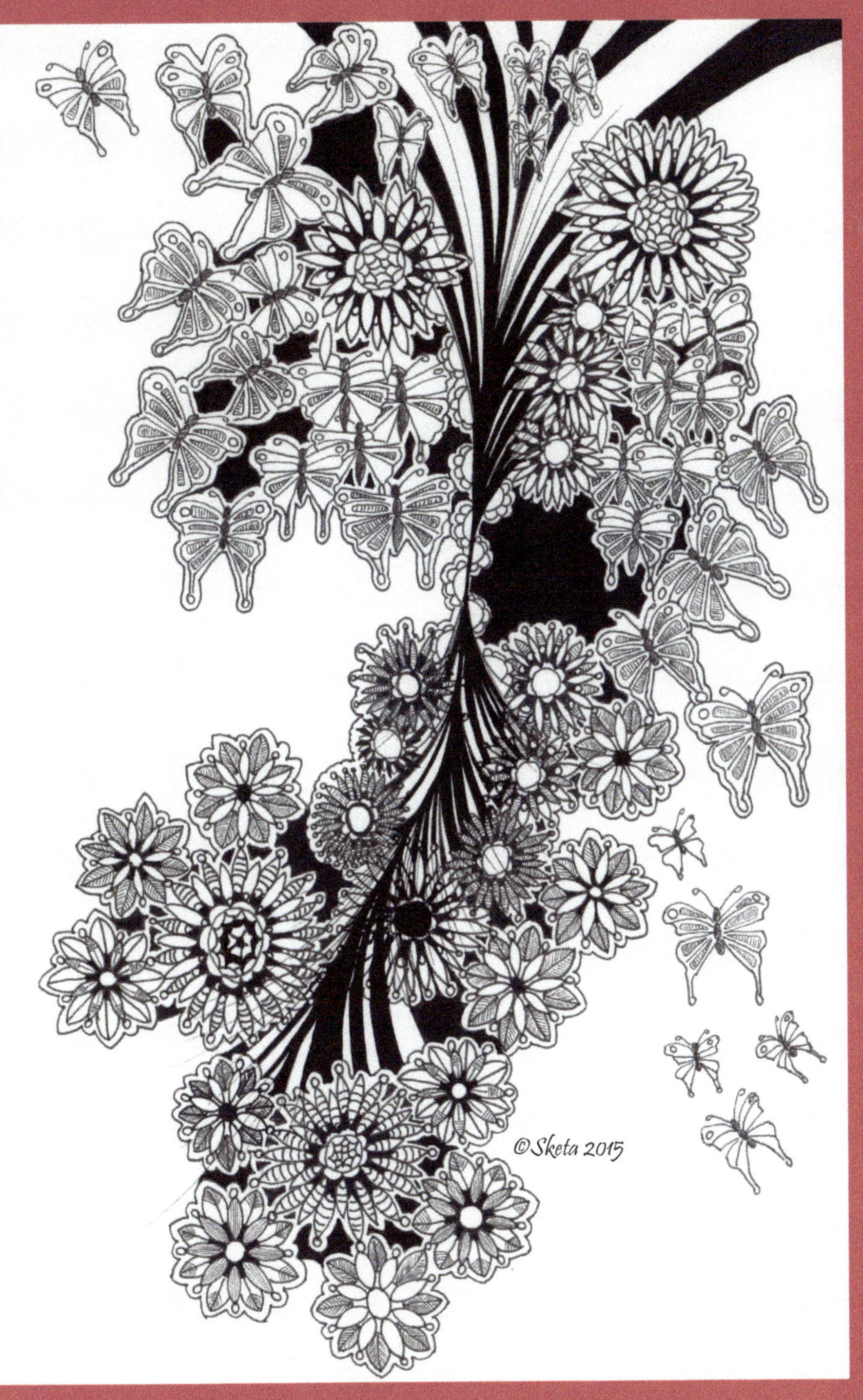
©Sketa 2015

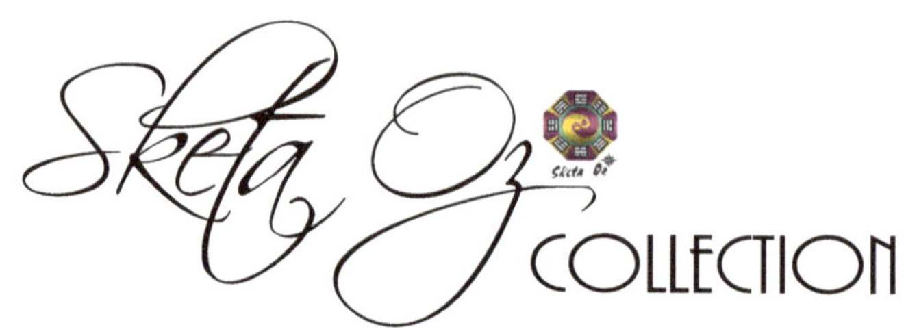

2016

BLACK & WHITE SERIES

(An Artist's Collection to Frame or Colour)

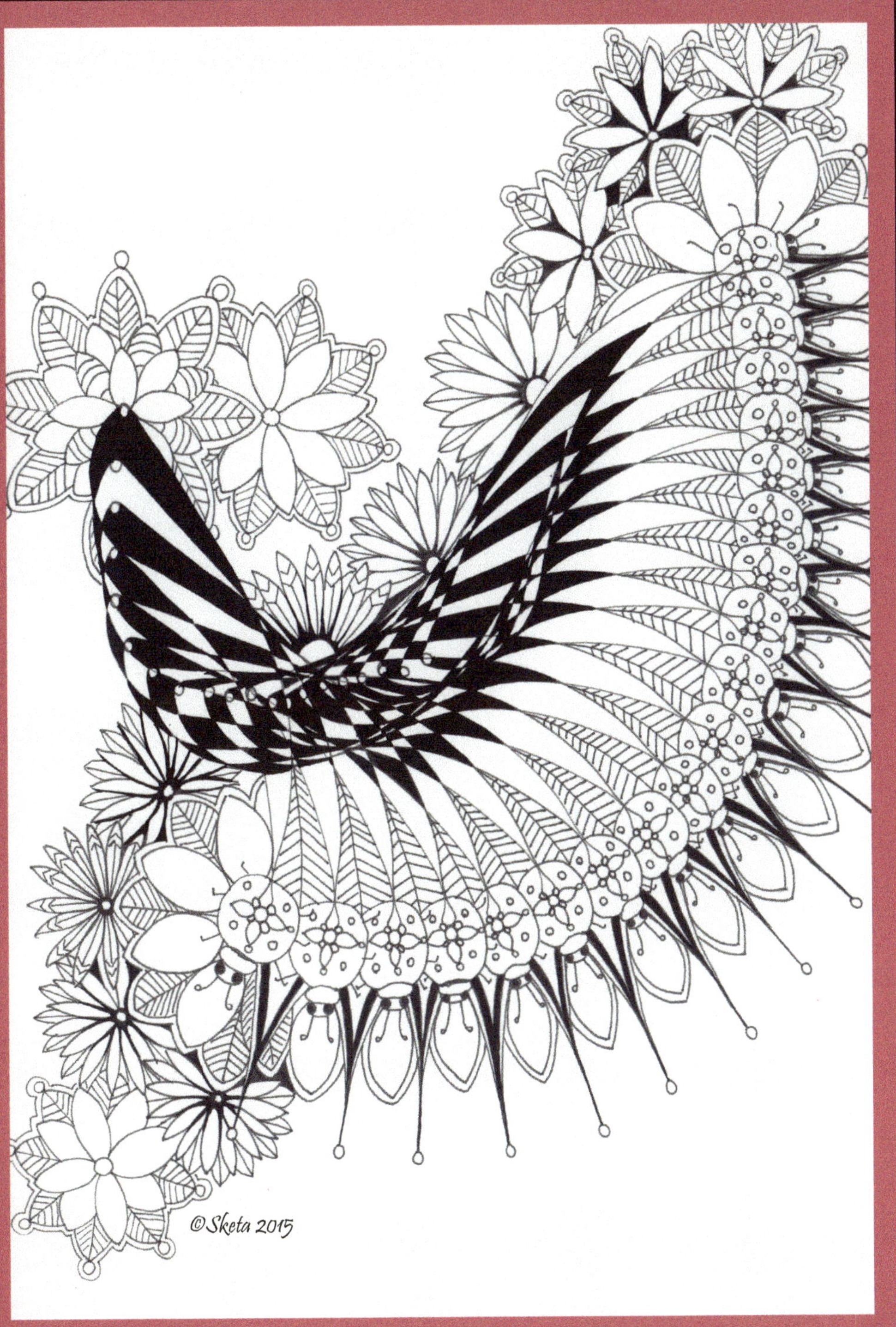
©Sketa 2015

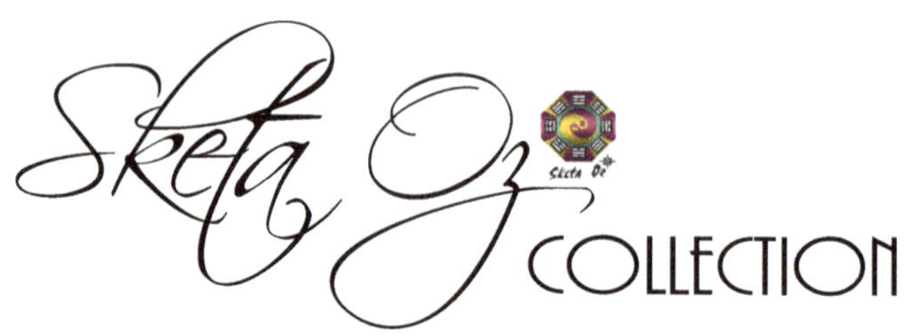

2016

BLACK & WHITE SERIES

(An Artist's Collection to Frame or Colour)

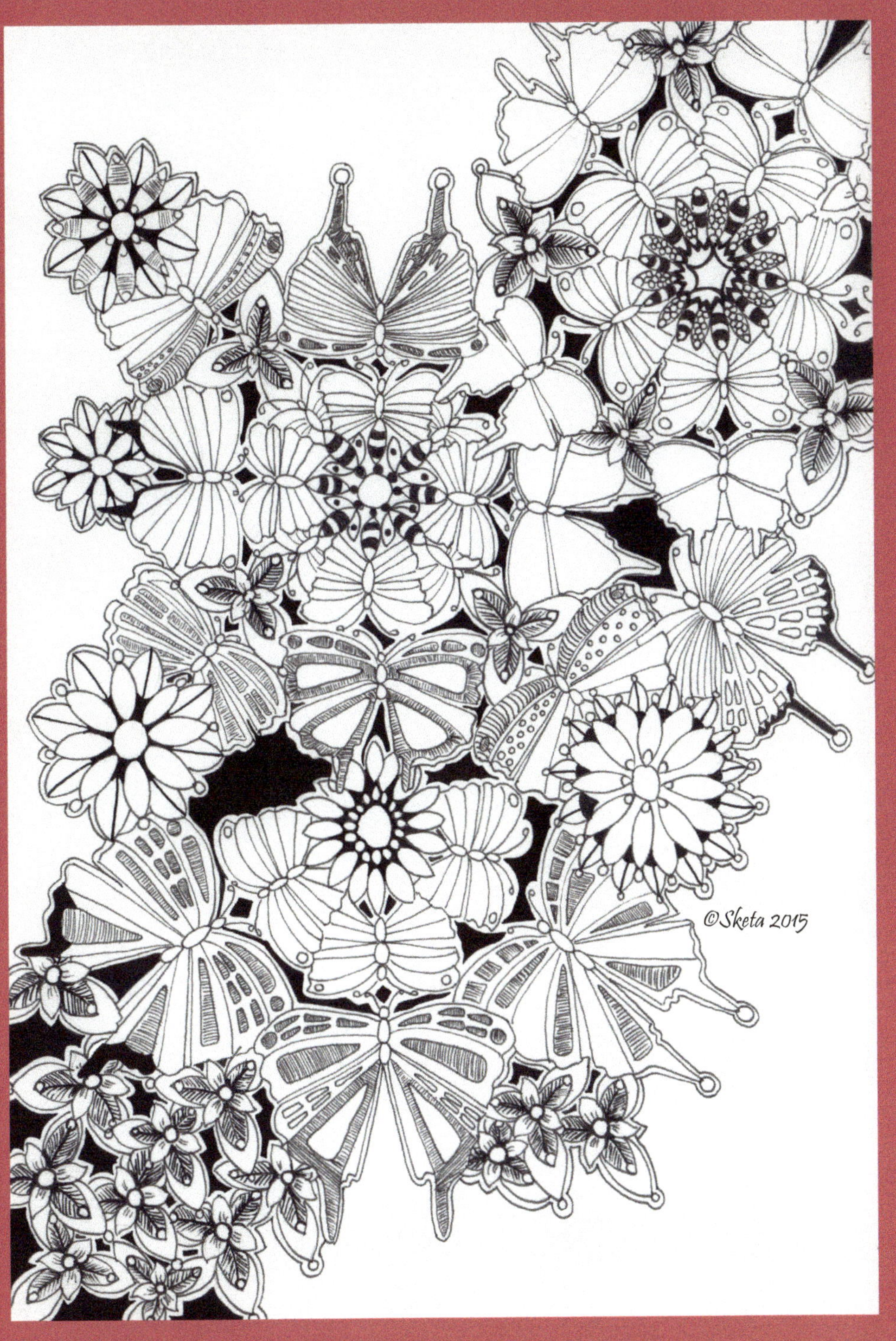
©Sketa 2015

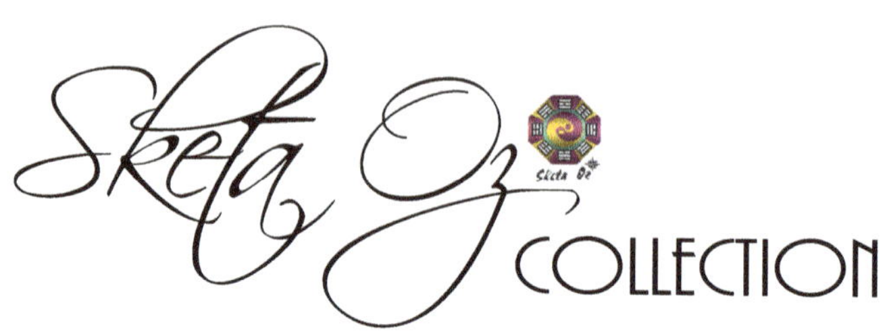

2016

BLACK & WHITE SERIES

(An Artist's Collection to Frame or Colour)

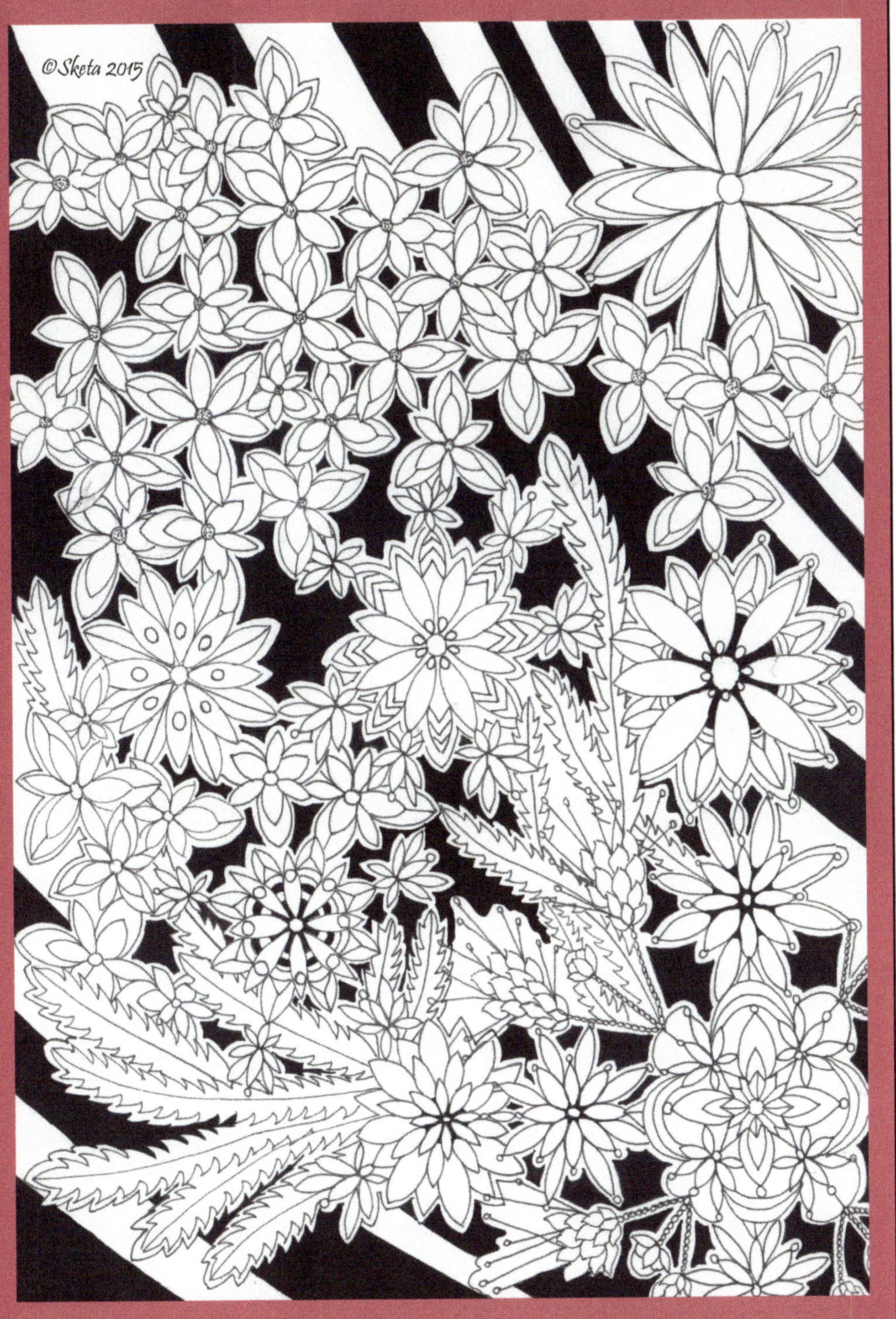
©Sketa 2015

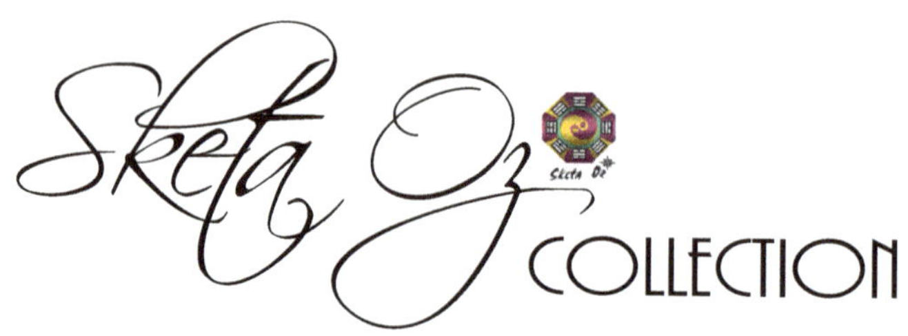

2016

BLACK & WHITE SERIES

(An Artist's Collection to Frame or Colour)

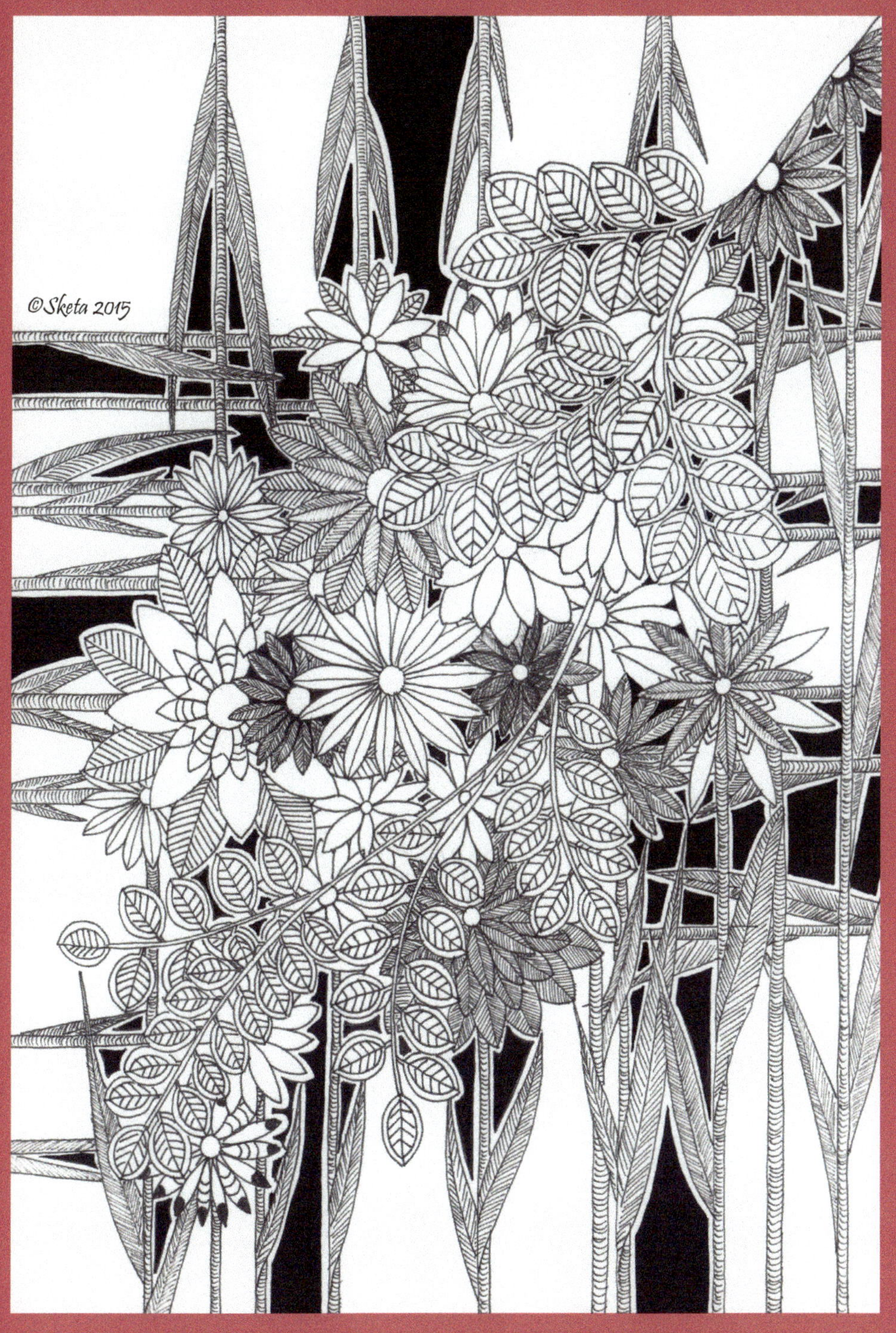
©Sketa 2015

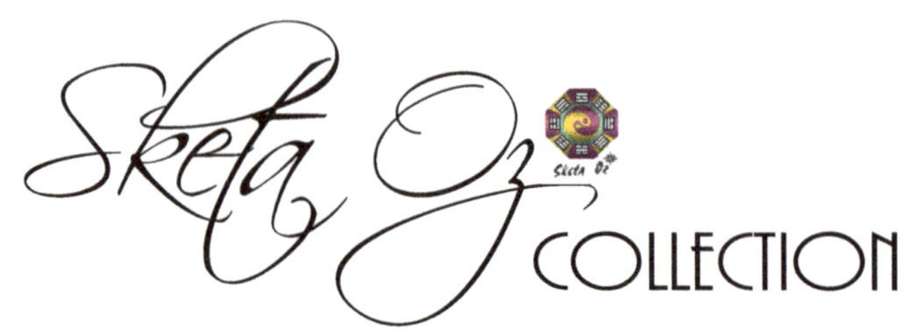

2016

BLACK & WHITE SERIES

(An Artist's Collection to Frame or Colour)

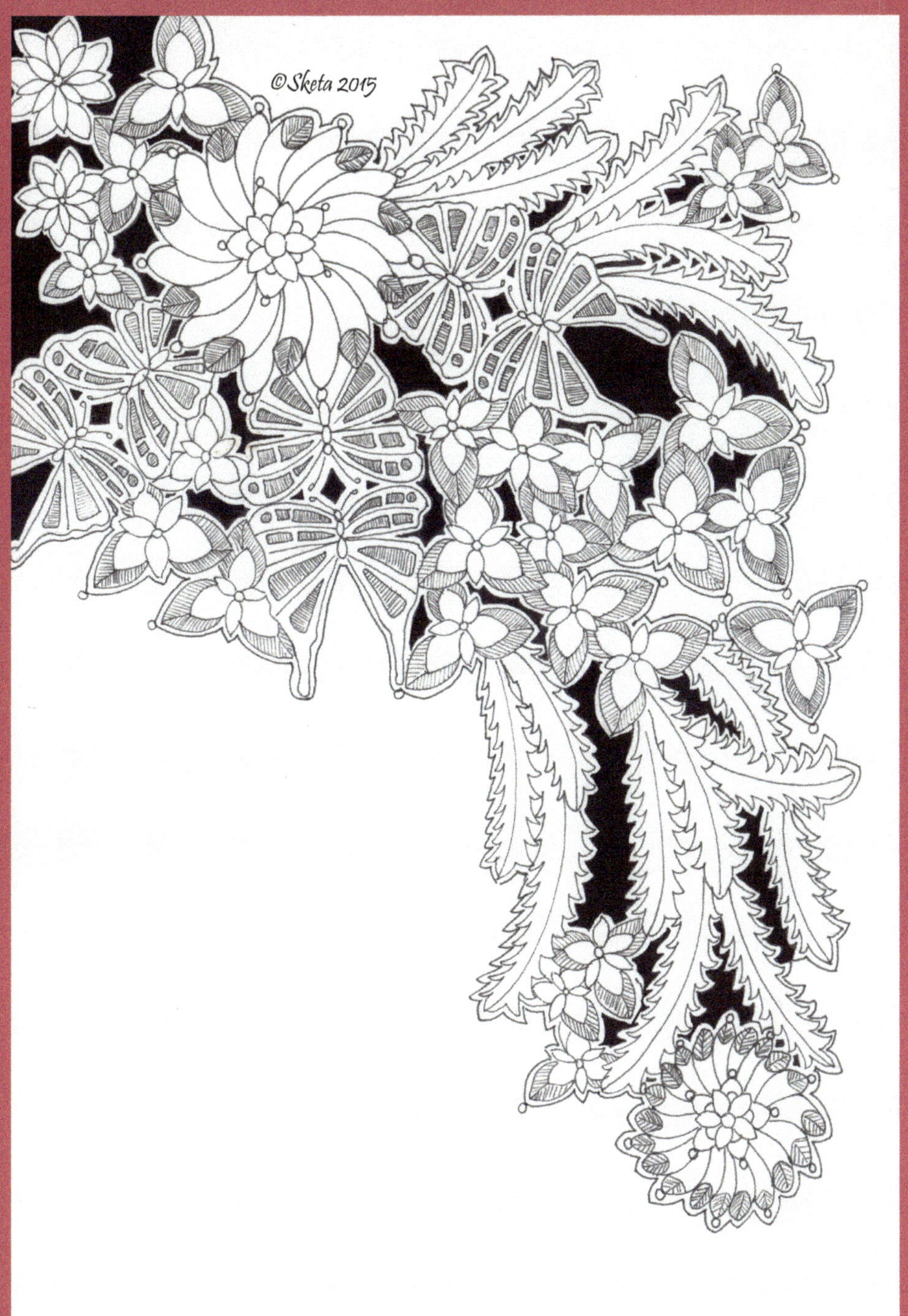
©Sketa 2015

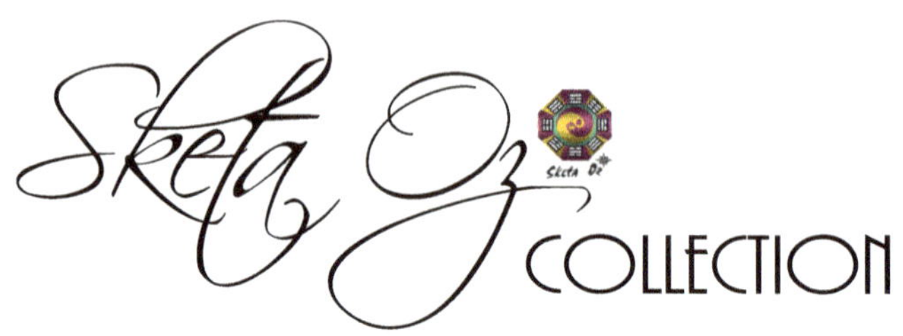

2016

BLACK & WHITE SERIES

(An Artist's Collection to Frame or Colour)

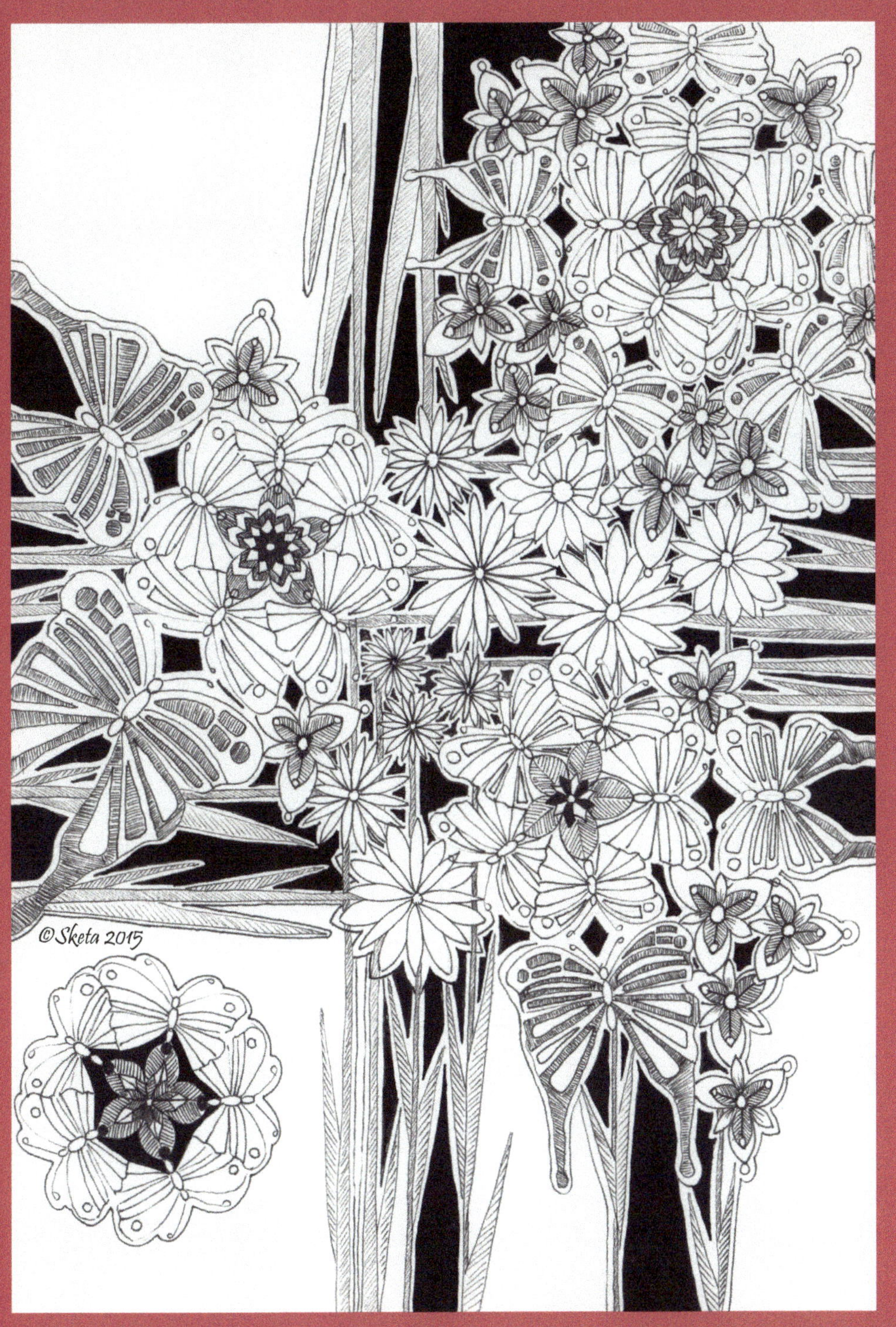
©Sketa 2015

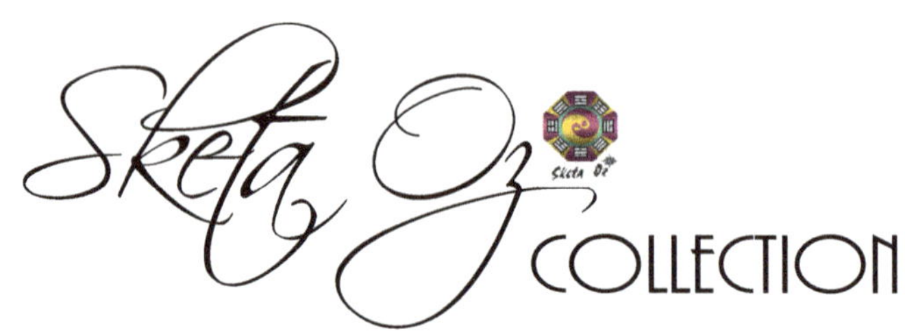

2016

BLACK & WHITE SERIES

(An Artist's Collection to Frame or Colour)

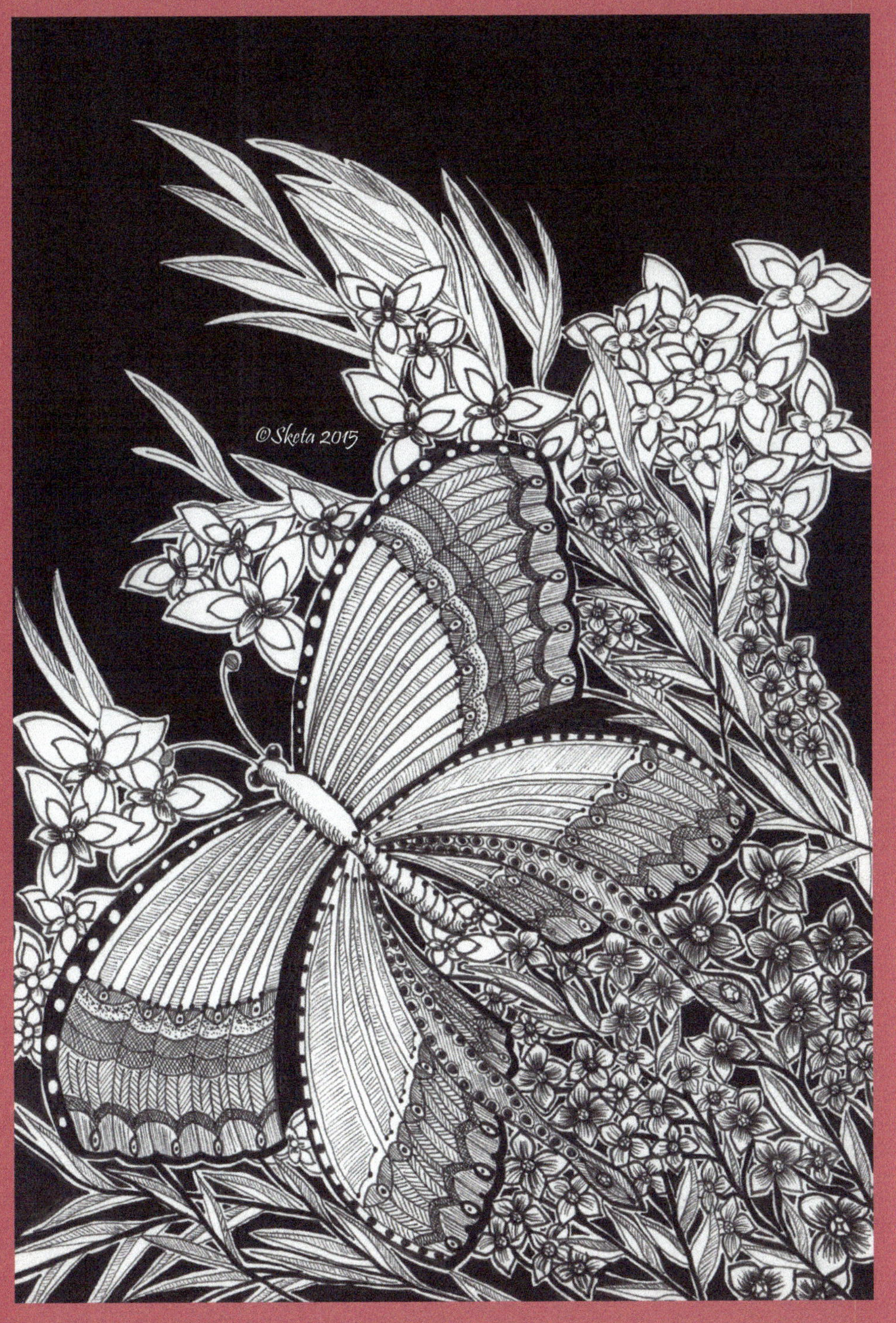
©Sketa 2015

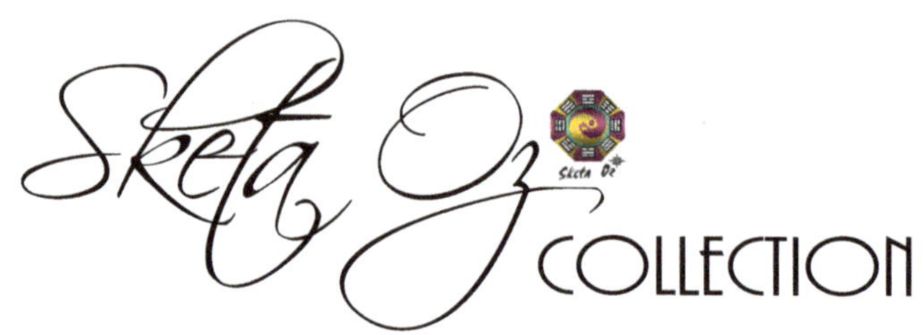

2016

BLACK & WHITE SERIES

(An Artist's Collection to Frame or Colour)

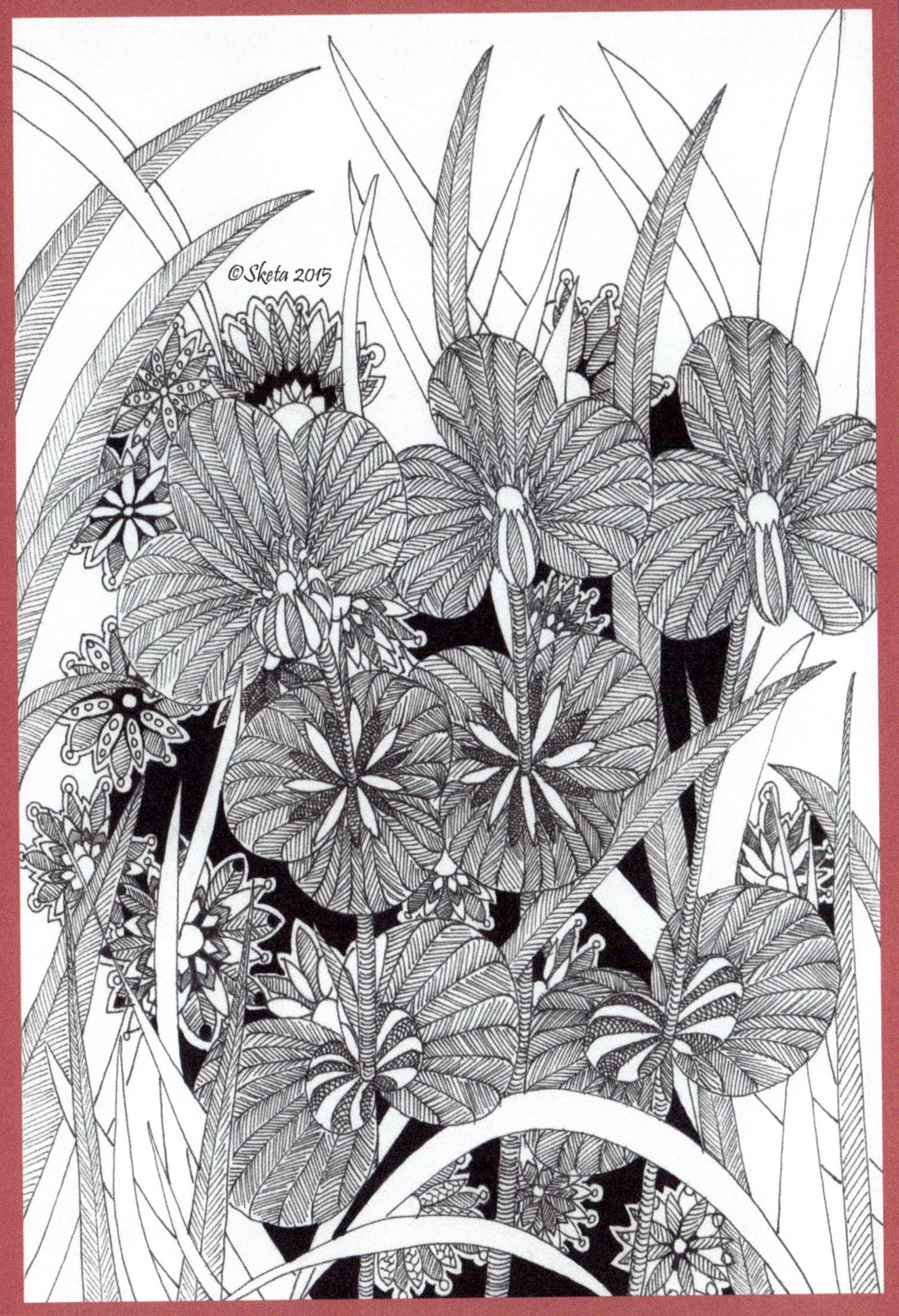
©Sketa 2015

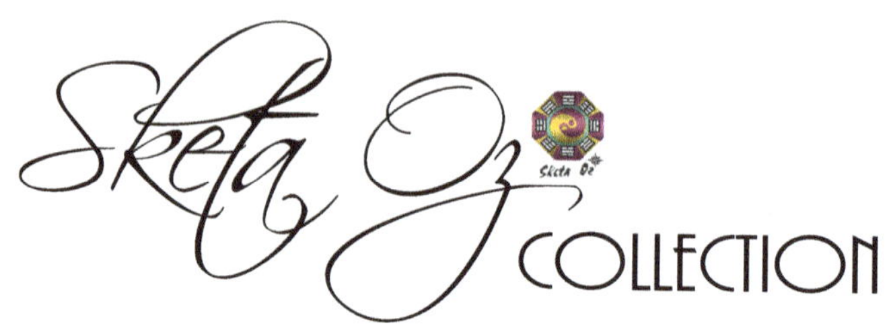

2016

BLACK & WHITE SERIES

(An Artist's Collection to Frame or Colour)

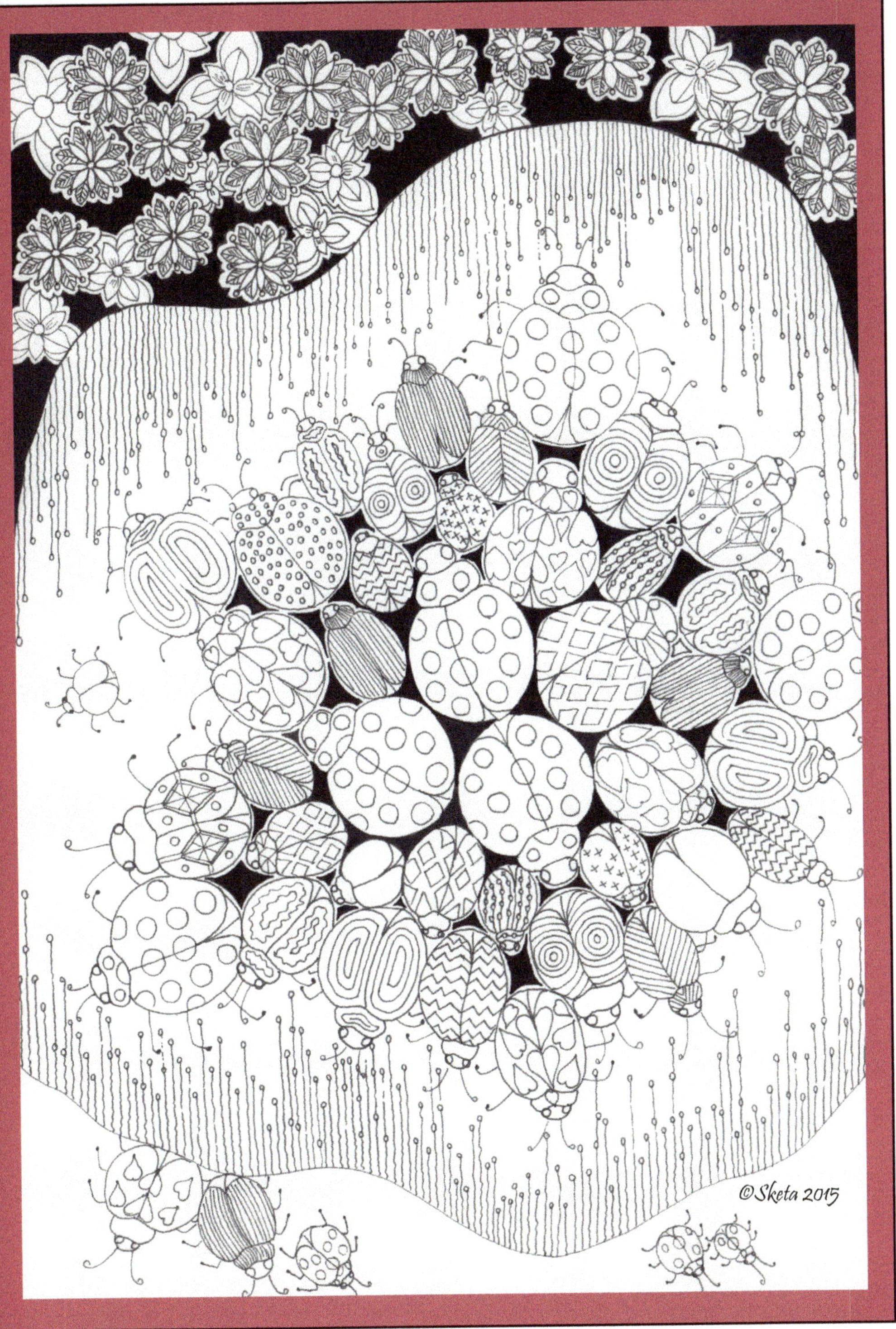
©Sketa 2015

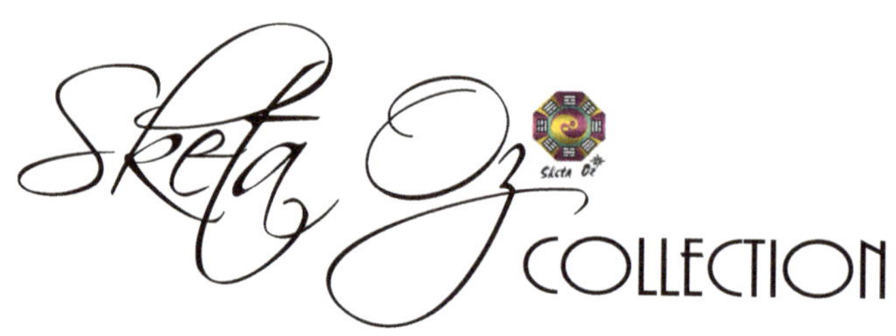

2016

BLACK & WHITE SERIES

(An Artist's Collection to Frame or Colour)

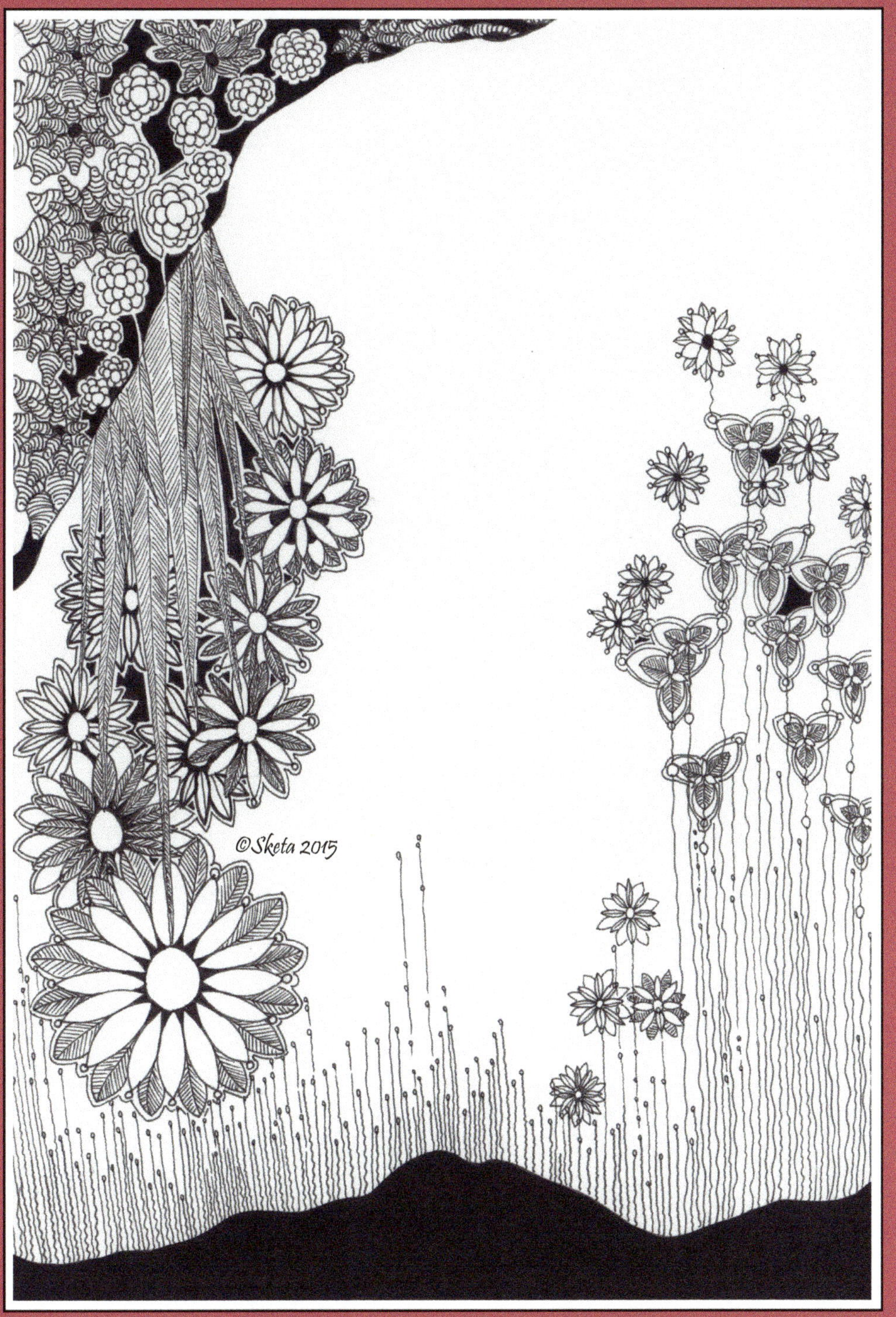
©Sketa 2015

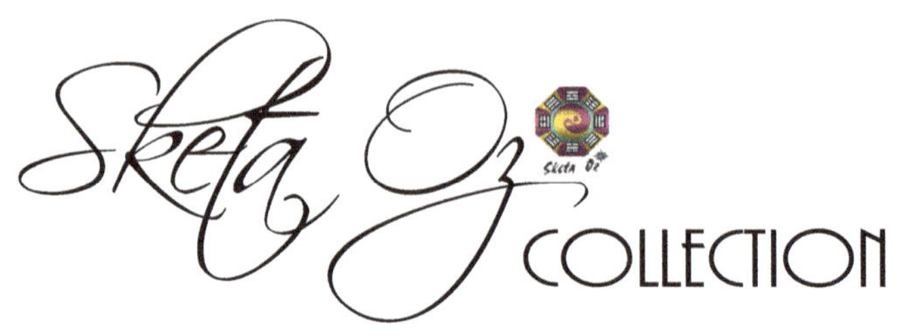

2016

BLACK & WHITE SERIES

(An Artist's Collection to Frame or Colour)

www.ingramcontent.com/pod-product-compliance
Ingram Content Group UK Ltd.
Pitfield, Milton Keynes, MK11 3LW, UK
UKHW062308290726
14090UKWH00018B/939